Theory of Music Grade 3
May 2016

CW00496206

Your full name (as on appointment form). Please use BLOCK CAPITALS.

_____

Your signature

_____

Centre

_____

Registration number

_____

Examiner's use only:

1 (10)	
2 (15)	
3 (10)	
4 (15)	
5 (15)	
6 (15)	
7 (20)	
Total	

(A-03)

Boxes
exami
use on

Section 1 (10 marks)

Put a tick (✓) in the box next to the correct answer.

Example

Name this note:

A ☐   D ☐   C ☑

This shows that you think **C** is the correct answer.

1.1   Name the circled note:

A ☐   F# ☐   D ☐

1.2   Add the total number of minim beats of **silence** in these bars.

3 ☐   4 ☐   5 ☐

1.3   Which is the main beat in $\frac{9}{8}$ time?

 ☐   ☐   𝅘𝅥. ☐

1.4   The relative minor of D major is:

B minor ☐
D minor ☐
G minor ☐

1.5   Which rest(s) would you put below the asterisk (*)?

𝄼. ☐   𝄾 ☐   𝄾𝄾 ☐

2

TRINITY
COLLEGE LONDON

2016
Grade 3

Theory of Music
Past Papers – 2016

Grade 3

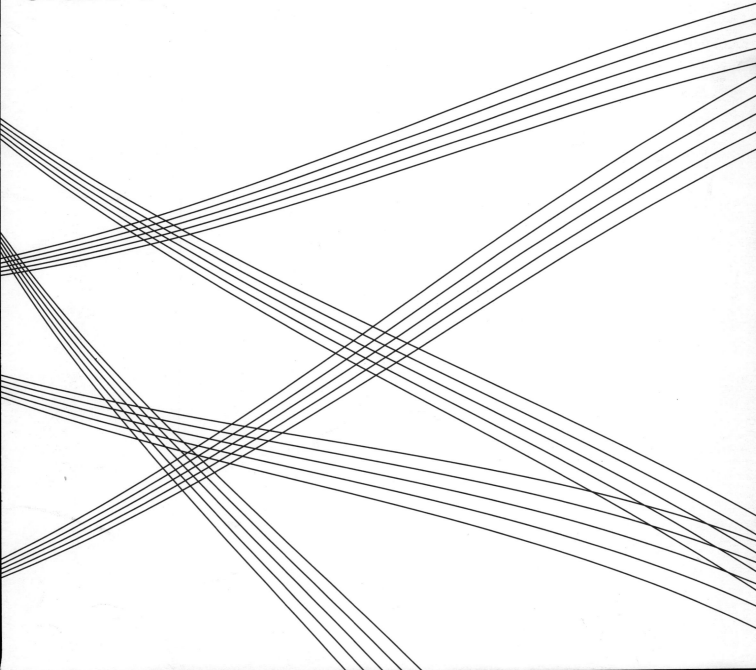

Put a tick (✓) in the box next to the correct answer.

1.6   Which note is the tonic of the minor key shown by this key signature?

G ☐   E ☐   B ☐   ☐

1.7   Which chord symbol fits above this dominant triad?

Am ☐   F ☐   C ☐   ☐

1.8   Name this interval:

major 7th ☐
minor 7th ☐   ☐
major 6th ☐

1.9   What does **alla** mean?

but ☐
little ☐   ☐
like ☐

1.10   Name this triad:

tonic triad of F major in second inversion ☐
tonic triad of A minor in second inversion ☐   ☐
tonic triad of A minor in first inversion ☐

Please turn over for Section 2

Boxes
exami
use or

Section 2 (15 marks)

2.1 Write a one-octave G melodic minor scale in minims, going up then down. Use the correct key signature and add any necessary accidentals.

2.2 Write the key signature shown. Then write its one-octave arpeggio in the rhythm given below.

D major, going up then down

Section 3 (10 marks)

3.1 Circle five different mistakes in the following music, then write it out correctly.

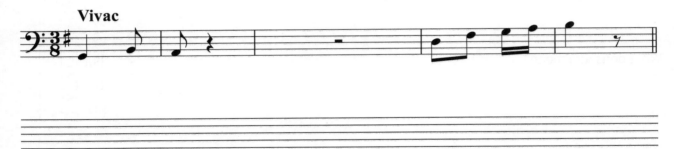

Section 4 (15 marks)

4.1 Transpose this tune up an octave into the treble clef to make it suitable for a violin to play.

Bach (adapted)

etc.

Section 5 (15 marks)

5.1 Using minims, write out 4-part chords for SATB using the chords shown by the Roman numerals.
Double the root in each case and make sure that each chord is in root position.

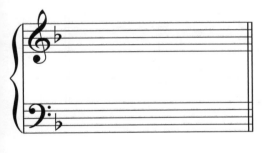

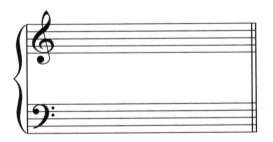

(F major)   I

(A minor)   i

Section 6 (15 marks)

6.1 Write the root of each triad shown by the chord symbols to write a bass line.

Please turn over for Section 7

Section 7 (20 marks)

Look at the following piece and answer the questions opposite.

Louis Raffy

Boxes for
examiner's
use only

7.1   In which key is this piece? _____

7.2   Which note is the leading note in this piece? _____

7.3   What does **Marziale** mean? _____

7.4   Name the interval between the two notes marked with asterisks (*) in bars 1 and 2.

_____

7.5   Name the cadence that ends this piece. _____

7.6   Put a bracket (⌐⌐) above one bar where the treble and bass parts move entirely in contrary motion.

7.7   What does *cresc.* mean? _____

_____

7.8   Write a Roman numeral below the first beat of bar 7 to show that the dominant chord
       accompanies the tune here.

7.9   What is the shortest note value used in this piece? _____

7.10   Is the sequence in bars 9–12 real or tonal (bass part)? _____

Theory of Music Grade 3
November 2016

TRINITY
COLLEGE LONDON

Your full name (as on appointment form). Please use BLOCK CAPITALS.

_____

Your signature   Registration number

_____   _____

Centre

_____

Instructions to Candidates

1. The time allowed for answering this paper is **two (2) hours.**

2. Fill in your name and the registration number printed on your appointment form in the appropriate spaces on this paper, and on any other sheets that you use.

3. **Do not open this paper until you are told to do so.**

4. This paper contains **seven (7) sections** and you should answer all of them.

5. Read each question carefully before answering it. Your answers must be written legibly in the spaces provided.

6. You are reminded that you are bound by the regulations for written exams displayed at the exam centre and listed on page 4 of the current edition of the written exams syllabus. In particular, you are reminded that you are not allowed to bring books, music or papers into the exam room. Bags must be left at the back of the room under the supervision of the invigilator.

7. If you leave the exam room you will not be allowed to return.

Examiner's use only:

1 (10)	
2 (15)	
3 (10)	
4 (15)	
5 (15)	
6 (15)	
7 (20)	
Total	

(C-03)

Boxes
exami
use or

Section 1 (10 marks)

Put a tick (✓) in the box next to the correct answer.

Example

Name this note:

A ☐   D ☐   C ☑

This shows that you think **C** is the correct answer.

1.1   Name the circled note:

G ☐   Bb ☐   F ☐

1.2   Add the total number of quaver beats in these tied notes:

7 ☐   8 ☐   9 ☐

1.3   Which time signature is in compound time?

$\frac{3}{4}$ ☐ $\frac{6}{8}$ ☐   ¢ ☐

1.4   Which rest(s) would you put below the asterisk (*)?

𝄽· ☐   ⁊ ☐   ⁊⁊⁊ ☐

1.5   The relative minor of Bb major is:

Bb minor ☐

G minor ☐

D minor ☐

Put a tick (✓) in the box next to the correct answer.

1.6   Name this interval:

major 2nd ☐
major 3rd ☐
minor 2nd ☐

☐

1.7   Here is the scale of A natural minor. Which degree(s) of the scale will you change to make the scale of A harmonic minor?

1   2   3   4   5   6   7   8(1)

6th degree ☐
7th degree ☐
6th & 7th degrees ☐

☐

1.8   Which chord symbol fits above this dominant triad?

Dm ☐
Bm ☐
D ☐

☐

1.9   What does **non** mean?

not ☐
more ☐
less ☐

☐

1.10   Name this triad:

tonic triad of B minor in root position ☐
tonic triad of B minor in first inversion ☐
tonic triad of D major in first inversion ☐

☐

Please turn over for Section 2

3

Section 2 (15 marks)

2.1 Write a one-octave B melodic minor scale in minims, going up then down. Do not use a key signature, but write in any necessary accidentals.

2.2 Using quavers, write a broken chord using F major tonic triad (going up). Use patterns of four notes each time and finish on the first **F** above the stave.

Section 3 (10 marks)

3.1 Circle five different mistakes in the following music, then write it out correctly.

Section 4 (15 marks)

4.1 Transpose this tune down an octave into the bass clef to make it suitable for a bassoon to play.

Bach

Section 5 (15 marks)

5.1 Using minims, write out 4-part chords for SATB using the chords shown by the Roman numerals. Double the root in each case and make sure that each chord is in root position.

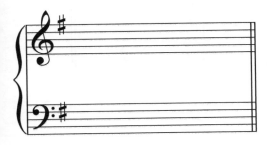

(E minor)   i

(B♭ major)   I

Section 6 (15 marks)

6.1 Use the root of each triad shown by the chord symbols to write a bass line.

Section 7 (20 marks)

Look at the following piece and answer the questions opposite.

Kirchner

7.1   In which key is this piece? _____

7.2   Which note is the dominant in this piece?_____

7.3   Write a Roman numeral below the last note of this piece to show that the tonic chord
       accompanies the music here.

7.4   Does the music start on an up-beat or a down-beat? _____

7.5   Look at bars 7–8: does the music move in similar or contrary motion? _____

7.6   What does *leggiero* mean?_____

7.7   Name the interval between the two notes marked with asterisks (*) in bars 11–12.

       _____

7.8   What is the pitch name of the last note in bar 4 (lower stave)? _____

       _____

7.9   Look at the boxed notes in bars 6–7. What do you notice about the pitch? _____

       _____

7.10   What does **Vivace** mean?_____

Theory of Music Past Papers – 2016
for Trinity College London written exams

This booklet contains two past exam papers for Trinity College London's Grade 3 exam in music theory, taken from exams sat in 2016.

Also available

In addition to past papers, Trinity publishes a range of support materials ideal for use in exam preparation. Model answer papers contain the correct answers, or those which would attract the highest marks. The Theory of Music Workbook series contains all the requirements of the graded exams and provides step-by-step instructions, suitable for use in lessons or for private study.

The following related publications are available from trinitycollege.com/shop or your local music shop:

Theory Model Answer Papers 2016 Grade 3   TCL 016386   ISBN 978-0-85736-578-1
Theory of Music Workbook Grade 3   TG 006523   ISBN 978-0-85736-002-1

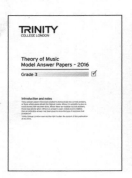
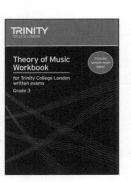

All syllabuses and further information about Trinity College London can be obtained from
trinitycollege.com

TCL 016461
ISBN 978-0-85736-586-6

9 780857 365866

TRINITY
COLLEGE LONDON